PEEK

Jeannie

enjoy the PEEK a~

Jeanne Martin Smith

· 2023·

PEEK

Come take a PEEK ... Fêtes and Fun...Family and Friends

Jeanne Martin Smith

gatekeeper press

Columbus, Ohio

PEEK

Published by Gatekeeper Press
2167 Stringtown Rd, Suite 109
Columbus, OH 43123-2989
www.GatekeeperPress.com

The cover design, interior formatting, typesetting, and editorial work for this book are entirely the product of the author. Gatekeeper Press did not participate in and is not responsible for any aspect of these elements.

ISBN (paperback): 9781662933264

One day while thinking about all the things I love ~ T H I S idea was born!

I love art
I love flowers
I love setting the table
I love cooking dinner
I love making desserts
I love photography
I love design and layout
I love ballet
I love my friends
I love my family
I love my home!

I dedicate this book to my husband Mark...my biggest supporter! He thinks everything I do is the BEST!...I think he is beyond wonderful!

...and to all my children and their families who fill my life with love and happiness and endless JOY!

San Diego  CALIFORNIA

My first party memory was on Leroy Street, the street where I grew up. The birthday party was for both my sister Judy and myself. My Avo' and mom made birthday hats for all our friends out of paper plates.... our brother Jimmy dressed up as a fortune teller. He made up fortunes while using the decorative round sphere on our mom's coffee table as a gazing ball. His fortune telling costume was made from shawls and scarves found in mom's closet. Lots of birthday H A P P I N E S S in our own backyard!

LEROY STREET BIRTHDAY PARTY

Art + Flowers

Celebrations

Holidays

Love Through Food + Recipes

Outdoor

Tablescapes

Graphics + Doodles

Art + Flowers

Visual Treats~no words necessary

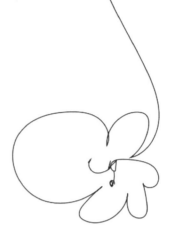

Celebrations

Celebrating Everything....

Festa do Espírito Santo
Madeira L O V E

Block- Buzzers News

Holidays

I REALLY love Christmas...

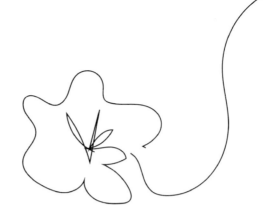

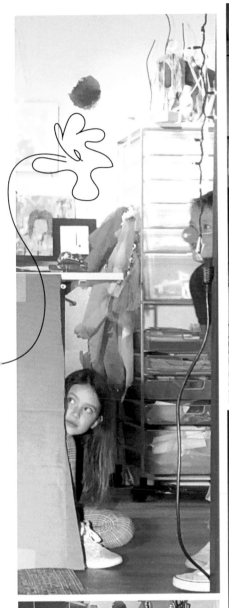

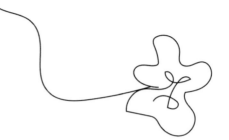

Love Through Food

Love through Food.. a seat at our table...

Recipes

SUGAR COOKIES

375 DEGREES BAKE 8-10 MINUTES

1/3 cup unsalted butter room temp
1/3 cup shortening
3/4 cup granulated sugar
1 egg
4 teaspoons whole milk
1 teaspoon pure vanilla extract
2 cups sifted unbleached white flour
1/4 teaspoon baking powder
1/2 teaspoon salt

Thoroughly cream butter, shortening and sugar in large mixing bowl. Add egg
and beat until light and fluffy. Add in milk and vanilla. Sift together flour,
baking powder and salt. Blend into creamed mixture until just comes together.
divide dough in half , wrap in waxed paper and chill for 1 hour.

Remove from refrigerator and roll out dough to 1/2 inch on lightly floured
surface. I usually roll between two pieced of waxed paper.

Cut with cookie cutter, flouring the cookie cutter as you go. I always use
a little flour under a spatula to lift the cut out cookies onto a cookie sheet
that has been light greased....or onto a silpat.

Bake for 8-10 minutes or until lightly browned. Cool and remove onto cooling rack.
Ice cooled cookies with powered sugar glaze and fun sprinkles or designs.

.

ICING

2 cups powdered sugar
3-4 Tablespoons water

Mix together to desired consistency. Color with food coloring if you like and add
Sprinkles while icing still wet.

ALMOND POUND CAKE WITH ORANGE GLAZE

325 DEGREES BAKE 1 HOUR

CAKE

5 ounces almond paste , grated
1 1/2 cups white granulated sugar
4 ounces unsalted butter, room temperature
4 large eggs...room temp
1 teaspoon orange zest
1 teaspoon pure vanilla
1/2 cup sour cream or greek yogurt
1 1/2 cups all purpose flour
1 teaspoon baking powder
1/2 teaspoon salt (if using unsalted butter)

GLAZE

1/3 cup powdered sugar
2 teaspoons orange juice

Preheat oven to 325°F. Grease the inside of a 5x9x3-inch loaf pan with butter or with non-stick spray.

Beat almond paste, add sugar, butter, eggs, zest, vanilla, yogurt:
Using a stand mixer, beat the almond paste, starting at a low speed.

Slowly add the sugar to the almond paste while beating, gradually increasing the speed, until incorporated.

Add the butter, and beat until fluffy, smooth, and almost white, about
5-6 minutes, on high speed.

Add the eggs, one at a time, beating a minute after each addition.

Beat in the orange zest, vanilla, and Greek yogurt.

Whisk dry ingredients:
In a medium bowl, vigorously whisk together the flour, baking powder, and salt.

Stir the flour mixture into the butter, almond paste, egg mixture:
a third at a time, until well blended.

Bake:
Pour batter into prepared loaf pan. Place on lower middle rack of your oven.

Bake at 325°F for 1 hour, until golden brown, and if you press down lightly
on the top it springs back at you, and a tester inserted into the center comes
out clean.

Cool for15 minutes...remove from pan and drizzle with glaze...add orange zest if you like.

Recipe by Simply Recipes via the internet with some adjustments made

HERB GRILLED QUAIL
SERVES 4 AS AN APPETIZER OR 2 AS A MAIN

4 Semi-Boneless Quail [I ordered mine from D'Artagnan]

1 teaspoon Dijon mustard
1 lemon, juice and zest
¼ cup olive oil
3 Tablespoons chopped fresh mixed herbs, we used tarragon, chives, thyme, and chervil
Kosher salt and freshly ground black pepper

Pat quail dry with paper towels, leave grill pins in. In a large bowl, whisk together
Dijon, lemon juice, lemon zest, and olive oil. Stir in herbs. Add quail, turning to coat
in the mixture. Cover and set aside for about 15 minutes. (The quail can be marinated
for up to 4 hours if desired, just cover and refrigerate until ready to cook. Bring birds
out of the fridge about 20 minutes before grilling.)
Preheat a lightly oiled grill to medium-high. Place the quail on the grill breast side
down, a few inches apart. Grill for about 3 minutes then carefully turn over and
continue to grill until birds are just cooked through, about 3-4 minutes more.
Remove to a platter to rest for 5 minutes. Serve with lemon wedges, if desired.

I love to serve this with Wild Rice, Caramelized Shallots and Corn Pudding.

This recipe is from D'Artagnan

CREAMY PASTA WITH FRESH HERBS

ABOUT 2 CUPS

CAMILLE'S FAVORITE!

4 Tablespoons unsalted butter
1 1/2 cups heavy cream
1/2 teaspoon kosher salt
1/8 teaspoon grated nutmeg
a pinch of cayenne pepper
1/4 cup Parmesan cheese
1 cup of finely chopped herbs
[my favorite combination: mostly basil, some mint, 3 chives]

Combine butter, cream, salt, nutmeg and cayenne pepper in a
heavy saucepan and simmer for 15 minutes or until sauce is
slightly reduced and a bit thickened.

Whisk in parmesan and fresh herbs and simmer another 5 minutes.
Taste and season to taste

Pour over your choice of pasta of choice and serve. Orzo or Angel Hair
pasta works great with this sauce.

...I have been making this for years...original recipe was
from The Silver Palate Cookbook

SCOTTISH SHORTBREAD

350 DEGREES   BAKE 45 MIN- 1 HOUR
FROM MY GRANDMA MARTIN

6 cups unbleached white flour
1 cup granulated sugar
1 pound unsalted butter...cold and cubed

Mix all together in food processor...or kitchen aid mixer until thoroughly
mixed. Pour into a jelly roll pan or cookie sheet wit sides. Press mixture
evenly over entire sheet pan. Bake 45 minutes to 1 hour in 350 degree
preheated oven until sides start to brown and come away from sides of pan.
Cool just 10 minutes in pan then cut into desired shapes while still hot.
You can prick with fork design on top at this time as well. Once cool
remove shortbread from pan and enjoy!

Shortbread can be frozen.

CHOCOLATE SNOWBALLS

375 DEGREES BAKE 8-10 MINUTES

2 & 2/3 cups unbleached flour
1/3 cup unsweetened cocoa [I use Hershey's]
3/4 cup sugar
1/2 pound [2 cubes] unsalted butter ...cut in cubes
2 egg whites [unbeaten]
1 teaspoon vanilla

1. Blend flour, cocoa, sugar and butter together in food processor.
2. Add egg whites and vanilla and process until forms a ball.
3. Chill dough 1 hour
4. Roll dough wit your hands into teaspoon size balls
5. Bake for about 10 minutes...until just done....do not overcook.
6. Cool for 5 minutes then drizzle using a teaspoon with white glaze....hold teaspoon above cookies and drizzle using back and forth motion.

GLAZE

2 cups powdered sugar
5 Tablespoons water

Mix all together to make a drizzle.
This can be as thick or thin as you like

BASQUE CHEESECAKE
400°F BAKE 50 MINUTES

2 1/4 pounds cream cheese, room temperature
1 3/4 cups sugar
1/4 teaspoon salt
5 large eggs..room temperature
2 cups heavy cream
1/4 cup all-purpose flour

.

Prepare a 10-inch spring form pan by covering the bottom with a piece of parchment
and then attaching and tightening the ring of the pan to hold the parchment in place.
Cut a strip of parchment taller than the pan and line the sides with it. Grease the
parchment lightly with butter or cooking spray.In a stand mixer, cream the cream
cheese and sugar on medium for about 5 minutes.Add salt and eggs one at a time
with the mixer on low.

Slowly add the heavy cream and finally the flour, and mix until fully incorporated.
It's crucial to scrape the bottom of the bowl with a spatula to incorporate any
cream cheese that may have gotten stuck.Pour batter into the prepared spring form pan

.

Bake for 50 minutes until medium-brown and nearly burned looking. The cake will still
have a bit of a wobble.Remove from oven and cool completely on a rack. The center
will drop, and a lip will develop on the edges.
Remove the spring form and serve

.

Serve at room temperature with lightly sweetened whipped
cream.....you can also serve with Rasberry Coulis.

ASPARAGUS WITH BLACK SESAME SEEDS

SERVES 8 AS A SIDE DISH

1 pound fresh asparagus
1 small garlic clove, minced
2-3 chive blossom heads
4-5 chives, chopped
3 Tblsp toasted sesame oil
1 Tblsp soy sauce
1 Tblsp black sesame seeds
a pinch of Kosher salt and freshly ground black pepper

Blanch asparagus for about 2 minutes in boiling water.
Remove quickly and bring down to room temp by rinsing in a cool water bath.
Drain well. In saute pan, saute sesame oil,with minced garlic, soy sauce and the
black sesame seeds for 1 minute.
Add chopped chives and toss in asparagus, moving around to coat the asparagus
fully. Place asparagus on a platter and drizzle over any remaining mixture in pan
on top of asparagus. Add a pinch of salt and pepper over top to taste.
Sprinkle the fresh chive blossoms on top.
You can serve immediately or also yummy at room temperature.

CHOCOLATE TRUFFLE CAKE
BAKE 425 DEGREES   BAKE 15 MINUTES
....FROM MY FRIEND FRAN

2 cups semi sweet chocolate chips
6 Tablespoons unsalted butter
2 Tablespoons sugar
2 teaspoons flour
1 teaspoon hot water
2 teaspoons pure vanilla
3 eggs, separated
pinch of salt

Melt chocolate chips and butter in double boiler. Mix in sugar, flour,
water and vanilla. Remove from heat and mix in yolks, one at a time. Cool.

Beat egg whites with salt until stiff but not dry.

Fold whites into cooled chocolate mixture.

Pour into buttered 8" spring form pan.

Bake at 425 degrees for 15 minutes. Do not overcook. The cake will be soft center
.
Cool on rack and serve with whipped cream, ice cream or your favorite caramel sauce.

MIMI'S OREOS
250 DEGREES   60 MINUTES

8 ounces cold unsalted butter cut in cubes
1/2 cup sugar
1 1/2 cups unbleached flour
pinch of salt
1/2 cup unsweetened cocoa powder

Combine butter and sugar in the bowl of an electric mixer. Mix on low speed
for 15-20 seconds using the paddle attachment. Add the flour, salt and cocoa
powder and continue mixing on low speed until dough starts coming together.
This will take 3-5 minutes. The dough will look dry until just before it all comes together.

Put the dough between two pieces of waxed paper and roll to about 1/4 inch thick
Use a round cookie cutter , cut and lift cookies onto a cookie sheet lined with a silpat.
I use a bit of flour on spatula when lifting the cookie rounds onto the cookie sheet.
At this point chill the whole cookie sheet with the cut our rounds in freezer for about
10 minutes.

Take cookie sheet out of freezer and bake at 250 degrees for 1 hour. Remove from
oven and let cool then lift cookies off with spatula and place on cooling rack
to cool completely.

Use 2 cookies for each sandwich ... fill with vanilla buttercream...
as much as you like between layers.*

VANILLA BUTTERCREAM

1/2 cup unsalted butter room temperature
1 1 lb. box Powdered sugar [about 3 1/2 cups]
1/2 teaspoon vanilla
3 Tablespoons milk
a pinch of salt

Mix all ingredients together until well blended.

*At Christmastime I will roll in crushed candy canes on sides where icing sticks out.

VANILLA CUPCAKES
350 DEGREES 16-18 MINUTES
MAKES 18 CUPCAKES

CAKE

1/2 cup unsalted butter ...room temp
1 1/2 cups sugar
2 1/2 cups unbleached flour
2 1/2 teaspoons baking powder
tiny pinch of salt
1 cup whole milk
1 teaspoon vanilla extract
1/4 teaspoon almond extract
4 egg whites stiffly beaten[about 1/2 cup]

Preheat oven to 350°F. Put cupcake papers in cupcake pan.

In large bowl [I use Kitchen aid Mixer] cream butter and shortening until light and fluffy.
In separate bowl sift together flour and baking powder,,,mix in salt. Mix dry ingredients
into creamed butter mixture adding slowly alternating with milk ...add in vanilla
and almond extract....and mix thoroughly. Fold in stiffly beaten egg whites.
Spoon into cupcake papers in cupcake pan filling each paper to about 3/4.
Bake in preheated oven for 16-18 minutes or until toothpick comes out clean.
Do not overbake Cool and frost..

.

ICING

1/2 cup unsalted butter
3 cups powdered sugar
1/8 teaspoon kosher salt
3-4 Tablespoons whole milk...or enough to make nice spreading consistency
Mix all together. Frost cupcakes when cool and add some fun sprinkles

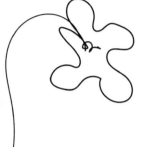

SUMMER PUDDING

1 pint fresh strawberries, hulled and sliced
1 1/2 cups sugar
3 half-pints fresh raspberries, divided
1 half-pint fresh blueberries

1 loaf brioche or egg bread [1 to 1-1/2 pounds]
Combine the strawberries, sugar, and 1/4 cup of water in a large saucepan
and cook uncovered over medium-low heat for 5 minutes. Add 2 cups of the
raspberries and all the blueberries and cook, stirring occasionally, until the
 mixture reaches a simmer, and simmer for a minute. Off the heat, stir in the
remaining raspberries.

Slice the bread in 1/2-inch-thick slices and remove the crusts. In the bottom
of a 7-1/2 inch round by 3-inch high soufflé or baking dish, ladle about
1/2 cup of the cooked berry mixture. Arrange slices of bread in a pattern
(this will become the top when it's unmolded) and then add more berry
mixture to saturate. Continue adding bread, cutting it to fit the mold,
and berries. Finish with bread and cooked berries, using all of the fruit and syrup.

Place a sheet of plastic wrap loosely over the pudding. Find a plate
approximately the same diameter as the inside of the mold and place
it on top. Weight the mold with a heavy can and refrigerate. Remove
the weight after 6 to 8 hours. Cover the pudding with plastic wrap and
refrigerate overnight.

Just before serving, run a knife around the outside of the pudding and
unmold it upside down onto a serving plate and serve with lots of
whipped cream....I use home whipped.

Original recipe from Ina Garten....some adjustments made

GOUGERES

400 DEGREES   BAKE ABOUT 20 MINUTES
ABOUT 40 CHEESE PUFFS

8 Tblsp. unsalted butter, chilled, cut into small pieces
a large pinch of sea salt
1 cup water
1 cup minus 1 Tblsp. unbleached flour
4 large eggs, lightly beaten
2 cups freshly grated Gruyère cheese

Line two baking sheets with silpats

In a medium heavy bottomed saucepan, combine the butter, salt
and water over high heat. Bring to a boil, whisking occasionally.
As soon as the mixture boils, remove from heat. Add the flour all at
once, and beat vigorously with a wooden spoon until the mixture
comes away from the sides of the pan. Return the pan to low heat
and continue beating for 1 minute, to dry out the dough.

Quickly transfer the dough to the bowl of a heavy duty electric
mixer fitted with a flat paddle. Gradually add the eggs and 1/2 cup
of the cheese, mixing at a moderately high speed to incorporate the
maximum amount of air. The dough should have the consistency of a
very thick mayonnaise.

Transfer the dough to a pastry bag fitted with a plain 1/2 inch tip.
Depending on the size of the bag this may have to be done in two batches.
Pipe into 2 inch mounds spacing them about 2 inches apart. If you don't
have a pastry bag, carefully spoon the dough onto the silpat lined baking sheets
with a teaspoon.

With a barely wet finger poke down the points on each mound, then
sprinkle tops with remaining cheese.

Place in center of the oven and bake until puffs are an even golden
brown. About 20 minutes. DO NOT OPEN OVEN DOOR to take
a peak while baking...your Gougeres will deflate and not puff up!

Remove from oven and cool for few minutes. These can be served
hot or at room temp.

...this is my go to recipe from the Simply French Cookbook by Patricia Wells

ORZO SALAD

SERVES 8

FROM MY FRIEND JILL FANUCCHI

1 1/2 cups orzo
1/3 cup oil packed sun dried tomatoes, drained and chopped
5 Tablespoons olive oil
1/4 cup balsamic vinegar
1/4 cup kalamata olives pitted and chopped

1 cup radicchio, finely chopped
1/2 cup toasted pine nuts
1/2 cup basil, chopped
1/2 cup Parmesan cheese, grated
2 large garlic cloves, minced

Cook orzo in pot of boiling lightly salted water until just tender but still firm. Drain well . Transfer to a large bowl. Add sun dried tomatoes, oil, vinegar and olives, toss to blend. Let stand until cool. Can be prepared 6 hours ahead, cover and refrigerate... bring to room temp before continuing. Mix chopped radicchio, pine nuts. chopped basil, Parmesan and garlic into orzo mixture. Season to taste with kosher salt and pepper. Serve and enjoy!

Outdoor

Outdoor....year round....

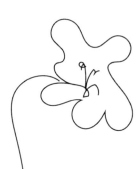

Tablescapes

A pretty table is a visual gift for your guests.....

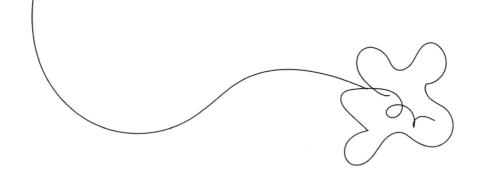

Graphic & Doodles

...doodles

PlayFUL Graphics....

Seas & GREETINGS

Carole's Apartment

Collioure

Collioure · France

Home and family are the center of my world! Our gatherings...big and small ...are much cherished traditions carried on with seeds planted by my parents and grandparents. I am so grateful that many of our children and grandchildren live nearby...and that they enjoy our gatherings as much as we do.

My grandmother taught me that time together is the very best gift we can give each other.

Deep Roots

...some of my Inspirers

Gloria Vanderbilt   @gloriavanderbilt

Annette Gomez   @flowersannettegomez

Philippa Craddock   @philippacraddock

Farmhouse Pottery   @farmhousepottery

Simon Pearce   @simonpearce

Susan Leader   @susanleaderpottery

Michele Coulon Dessertier   @dessertier

Azucar   @iloveazucar

Stray Dog   @straydogdesigns

Brooke Giannetti Patina Meadow   @velvetandlinen

Casa Gusto   @getthegusto

Lavanda Comporta   @lavandacomporta

Kerri Rosenthal   @kerri.rosenthal

Luke Edward Hall   @lukeedwardhall

Charlotte Moss @charmossny

Willow Crossley   @willowcrossleycreates

Jaques Grange   @jacques.grange

Carolina Irving and Daughters   @carolinairving_and_daughters

Monique Soares Kraft Interiors @interiorsmsk

Domaine de Manion   @bonniejomanion

Bill Bocken Architect   @billbocken

Georgia Macmillan   @gcmacmillan

Lisa Fine   @lisafinetextiles

Favorite stores San Diego

Bazaar del Mundo   @bazaardelmundo
The Faded Awning   @thefadedawning
The Portuguese Market   @theportuguesemarket
Lewis & Fay   @lewisandfay
en concordia   @enconcordia

Favorite store in California

The Well Summerland   @thewellsummerland
Molly Wood Garden Design   @mollywoodgarden
The FIND Consignments   @theFINDConsignments
Tancredi & Morgen   @tancredimorgen

I took my first Graphics Arts class at Point Loma High School. Back then I
was the only girl in the class. My teacher, Mr. Schaffroth welcomed me
with open arms. Many years later just for fun I signed up for a Typography
class. My professor was Candice Lopez. She completely drew me in
and I ended up taking every design class possible with Honors in Visual Arts.
I would like to thank both Mr. Schaffroth and Professor Lopez for
inspiring and feeding my lifelong love for everything related to design.

I would also like to thank those who planted the seeds to allow me
to blossom and bloom! My roots run deep ... thank you's go to my amazingly talented
Avo' Raquel, my dear sweet mother Mary ...my dad Otha and much cherished aunts,
uncles and cousins...also to this wonderful little community where I was born and raised.
And to my husband Mark and all my children and their families who have filled my
life with unconditional love and joy.

Family traditions and love are what inspire me to do everything I do!

...lucky me!